This Book Belongs To

_____

My Hebrew Name

_____

The Secular Date of My Bar/Bat Mitzvah Ceremony

_____

The Hebrew Date of My Bar/Bat Mitzvah Ceremony

_____

Name and Location of Synagogue

_____

_____

This Book Was Given to Me By

_____

66 When a Jewish child reads from the Torah, he or she is
enveloped in its heritage, in its power, in the majesty of Sinai.
He or she says to the community: 'I am now thirteen years old.
I am now ready to fulfill the covenant with God by being responsible
for performing *mitzvot,* the obligations of Jewish life.' **99**

—*Putting God on the Guest List*

The Bar/Bat Mitzvah Memory Book

An Album for
Treasuring the Spiritual Celebration
2nd Edition

RABBI JEFFREY K. SALKIN & NINA SALKIN

JEWISH LIGHTS Publishing
Woodstock, Vermont

Dedicated to our mothers, Sidonia Karpel Salkin, of blessed memory, and Isabelle Rubin, who never had the opportunity to become bat mitzvah. To our fathers, George Salkin and Mel Rubin, who were bar mitzvah and who wish that it had been a different kind of experience. To our sons, Sam and Gabriel, who are doing it "our way," and, we pray, "their way."

Acknowledgments

We appreciate all the hard work of Lauren Seidman, Sandra Korinchak, Martha McKinney, and Emily Wichland, who shepherded this project along. Our inspiration continues to be Stuart M. Matlins, publisher of Jewish Lights, who realized the need for this book and who invited us to create it.

We are deeply grateful to our summer Berkshires *havurah*—the Goldsteins, Karps, and Spungen-Bildner families. Over the past ten years, we have thought out loud together about our children's *b'nei mitzvah*, and we have dreamed together about a Jewish world where God, Torah, and *mitzvot* might assume center stage.

The Bar/Bat Mitzvah Memory Book, 2nd Edition:
An Album for Treasuring the Spiritual Celebration

2007 Second Edition, Second Printing
2006 Second Edition, First Printing
© 2006 by Jeffrey K. Salkin and Nina Salkin

Excerpts from *Putting God on the Guest List: How to Reclaim the Spiritual Meaning of Your Child's Bar or Bat Mitzvah; For Kids—Putting God on Your Guest List: How to Claim the Spiritual Meaning of Your Bar or Bat Mitzvah; I Am Jewish: Personal Reflections Inspired by the Last Words of Daniel Pearl; The Book of Jewish Sacred Practices: CLAL's Guide to Everyday & Holiday Rituals & Blessings; Tough Questions Jews Ask: A Young Adult's Guide to Building a Jewish Life;* and *The JGirl's Guide: The Young Jewish Woman's Handbook for Coming of Age* are reprinted by permission of Jewish Lights Publishing.

10 9 8 7 6 5 4 3 2

This book is printed on acid-free paper.
Manufactured in Hong Kong
Cover design: Bronwen Battaglia
Text design: Chelsea Cloeter
Cover art: Robert Lipnick

Published by Jewish Lights Publishing
A Division of LongHill Partners, Inc.
Sunset Farm Offices, Route 4, P.O. Box 237
Woodstock, VT 05091
Tel: (802) 457-4000   Fax: (802) 457-4004
www.jewishlights.com

Contents

Introduction: What Makes This Bar/Bat Mitzvah Memory Book
Different from All Other Memory Books?   5

Who Am I and What Am I? | 7 | מי אני ומה אני

Go Forth from the Land of Childhood | 15 | לך לך מארצך וממולדתך ומבית אביך

And This Is the Torah | 19 | וזאת התורה

From All My Teachers I Have Gained Wisdom | 25 | מכל מלמדי השכלתי

Come Before God with Rejoicing | 29 | באו לפניו ברננה

Joy and Gladness | 39 | שמחה וששון

Clear a Pathway through the Wilderness of Life | 45 | פנו דרך במדבר

Introduction

What Makes This Bar/Bat Mitzvah Memory Book Different from All Other Memory Books?

Recently our younger son, Gabriel, became bar mitzvah. It was a lovely ceremony and he did very well. It was a joy to have our community, family and friends celebrating with us. And yes, there was also that lump in our throats that contained its own message: The second and last child is now bar mitzvah. That's two down, none to go. Our sons are launched. We are no longer young parents. This is where middle age begins.

It was a bittersweet moment, but a sacred one as well. Our friend Joel Grishaver, Jewish educator and author, once advocated the idea of starting a Jewish photo album for each child. When your child is born, buy a photo album with empty plastic sheets. Create labels for each page: "First day at Jewish nursery school." "First day of religious school." "First time giving tzedakah." "Becoming bar/bat mitzvah." "Getting on the plane to Israel for the first time." And then, he said, take the pictures. You already have the pages labeled for them. Just live your Jewish life in a way that you will be able to witness those scenes and remember them.

That's what makes this bar/bat mitzvah memory book different from all other memory books.

It is an exercise in "pre-memory." Parents, by looking through the pages in this book, and seeing the kinds of memories your child might have and might consider worth remembering forever, you and your child can actually plan those experiences and, therefore—if such a thing is possible—"plan" those special feelings of memory that will endure. Because those memories are, in fact, holy.

This is your road map for bar/bat mitzvah. It will help you know what to expect and what the major holy sites are on the sacred journey through this important moment of Jewish life. It will help you not to miss the spiritual highlights of bar/bat mitzvah—highlights that can be kept alive each day of your life after the ceremony.

Many families are looking for ways to make the bar/bat mitzvah experience richer and deeper. To help you do that, you may wish to use this book along with *Putting God on the Guest List: How to Reclaim the Spiritual Meaning of Your Child's Bar or Bat Mitzvah* and *For Kids—Putting God on Your Guest List: How to Claim the Spiritual Meaning of Your Bar or Bat Mitzvah* (both published by Jewish Lights). You will learn how to plan to remember the significant moments in this sacred rite of passage.

We once knew a religious school teacher who had a family Bible with the names of everyone in the family inscribed in it—going all the way back to 1400s Spain! Imagine how you would feel if your own ancestors had kept a careful record of everyone in their own families. With this memory book, you can create a keepsake that will become a family heirloom to last through the years.

This memory book will help you see yourself as part of a rich history that includes your family and that goes beyond your family. The Hebrew term for memory, *zachor*, is used 169 times in the Torah. The square root of 169 is 13, the age of becoming bar/bat mitzvah. Memory is the square root of everything we do in Jewish life.

Mazal tov!

Rabbi Jeffrey K. Salkin   Nina Salkin

Who
Am I
and
What
Am I?

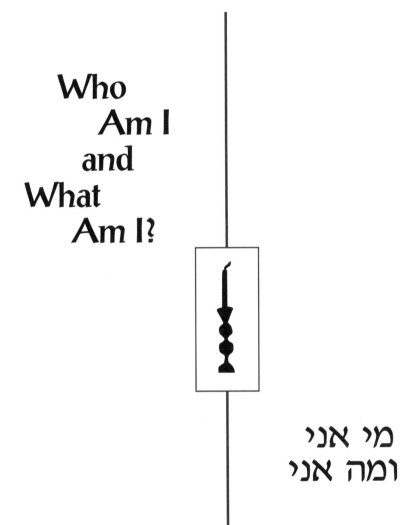

מי אני
ומה אני

❝ There is no such thing as a bar or bat mitzvah ceremony
without tears.

The tears belong to several people.
They belong to parents who are swelling with pride and relief.

They belong to grandparents who may come up for their *aliyah.*
They listen to their grandchild read or chant from the Torah,
and by the time they utter the closing blessing,
their lips are quivering and their tears are falling.

I have seen tears fall right onto the Torah scroll.

Of all the places where tears might fall,
that is the holiest place of all. **❞**

—*Putting God on the Guest List*

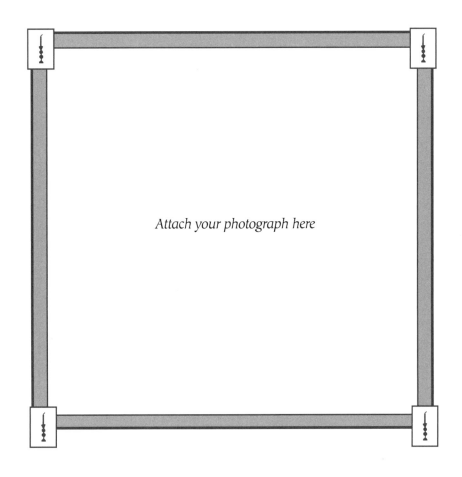

Attach your photograph here

I am named for:

_____   _____
NAME/RELATION   NAME/RELATION

These are their qualities that I would like to emulate:

_____   _____

_____   _____

My name means:

_____

My Family

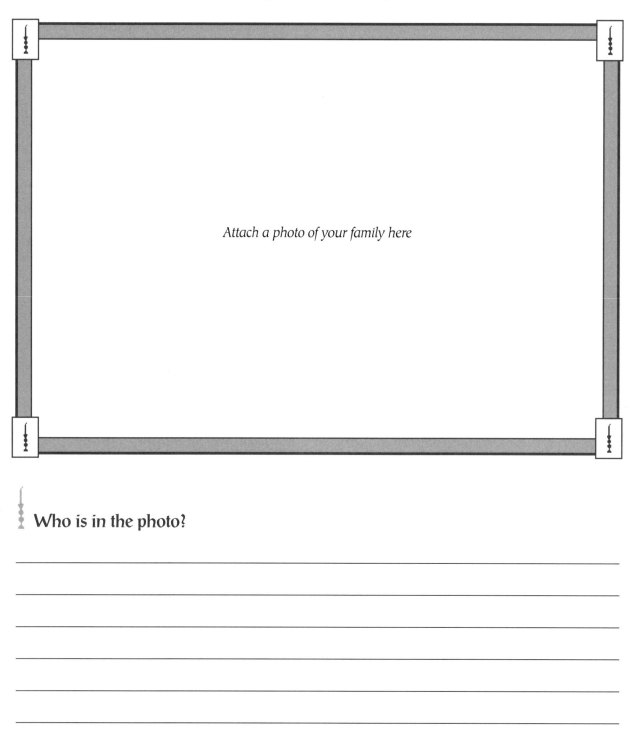

Attach a photo of your family here

Who is in the photo?

_____

_____

_____

_____

_____

_____

_____

My Family Tree

Draw your family tree and attach it here

66 We believe, pray, and are
because our parents and grandparents,
and their parents and grandparents,
believed, prayed and were.**99**

—Menachem Rosensaft, in *I Am Jewish*

66 These are the names
of the children of Israel ...**99**

—Exodus 1:1

What do my relatives (parents, grandparents, aunts, uncles, etc.) remember about when they became bar or bat mitzvah?

_____ remembers:
NAME OF RELATIVE

The name of the synagogue: _____

It was located in: _____ Date of the ceremony: _____

The names of the rabbi, cantor, or other people
who helped them prepare for their bar or bat mitzvah: _____

_____

The Torah portion: _____

Special memory of ceremony: _____

_____

_____

_____ remembers:
NAME OF RELATIVE

The name of the synagogue: _____

It was located in: _____ Date of the ceremony: _____

The names of the rabbi, cantor, or other people
who helped them prepare for their bar or bat mitzvah: _____

_____

The Torah portion: _____

Special memory of ceremony: _____

_____

_____

_____ remembers:

NAME OF RELATIVE

The name of the synagogue: _____

It was located in: _____ Date of the ceremony: _____

The names of the rabbi, cantor, or other people
who helped them prepare for their bar or bat mitzvah: _____

_____

The Torah portion: _____

Special memory of ceremony: _____

_____

_____

_____ remembers:

NAME OF RELATIVE

The name of the synagogue: _____

It was located in: _____ Date of the ceremony: _____

The names of the rabbi, cantor, or other people
who helped them prepare for their bar or bat mitzvah: _____

_____

The Torah portion: _____

Special memory of ceremony: _____

_____

_____

66 The Talmud teaches that
to hear your child's child reading Torah
is like hearing the words from Sinai itself. 99

—Putting God on the Guest List

This page is for you and your parents to fill out together.

יהי רצון מלפניך

Ye'he ratzon mil'fanekha

"May it be Your Will": that as I study and review Torah,
turning it and turning it and making it my own, I will find everything in it.

To keep perspective during the months before your bar or bat mitzvah, set a moment aside on the day your preparation officially begins and use the space below to write one sentence that will remind you of one spiritual goal you'd like to attain during this year of study and preparation. Invite your parent(s) to write one spiritual goal as well. Come back to this page often to keep track of your progress.

—*The Book of Jewish Sacred Practices*

My spiritual goal for the year ahead is:

_____

_____

My parent(s)' spiritual goals for the year ahead are: _____

_____

_____

66 When I became bar mitzvah,
my grandfather came to me one night
in a vision
and gave me another soul
in exchange for mine.
Ever since then,
I have been a different person. 99

—Shalom of Belz, Hasidic teacher

Go Forth
from the Land
of Childhood

לך לך מארצך
וממלדתך
ומבית אביך

66 Bar and bat mitzvah is about ritual maturity.
It is about growing up as a Jew.
It is about becoming a fuller member
of the Jewish community.
But it is also about moral responsibility,
about connecting to Torah, to community, to God. **99**

—*Putting God on the Guest List*

66 The bar/bat mitzvah ceremony…
means that you've begun the *process* of growing up.
You've started on the pathway to becoming an adult….
Everyone is given the chance to celebrate
the beginning of this amazing passage
from being a kid to becoming an adult. **99**

—*Tough Questions Jews Ask*

📖 Why am I having this ceremony?

_____

_____

_____

_____

📖 What do I want to remember about my bar/bat mitzvah experience?

_____

_____

_____

_____

📖 These are the *mitzvot* that I performed to prepare to become bar or bat mitzvah (see *For Kids—Putting God on Your Guest List* for a list of *mitzvah* project ideas):

_____

_____

_____

_____

_____

_____

_____

📖 I contributed to these *tzedakot* (see *Putting God on the Guest List* for a list of *tzedakot* ideas):

_____   _____

_____   _____

_____   _____

My parent(s) have special blessings for me.

They want me to always be proud to be Jewish because:

_____

_____

_____

_____

_____

_____

_____

_____

❝ May learning Torah be a source of joy for our children.
Help them to learn easily, to perform Your *mitzvot*,
and to be open to wisdom and insight.
May we support them as they wrestle,
discover, challenge, and delight.
May we watch them blossom in their learning. ❞

—*The Book of Jewish Sacred Practices*

❝ My parents are the instruments God used
to bring me into being.
Through trying to understand and listen to them,
I begin to comprehend myself. ❞

—Rabbi Lawrence Kushner, in *I Am Jewish*

And
This
Is
the Torah

וזאת
התורה

66 According to Midrash, all Jewish souls
        were present at Mt. Sinai, even those
                not yet born (*Exodus Rabbah* 28:4).
Everyone there received the Torah in their own way,
                according to their own understanding.
It is up to each individual to give their Torah,
                their personal wisdom, to the world. 99

—The JGirl's Guide

66 The Torah scroll is not vocalized
        to allow the wise to give his own voice to the text.
This is what keeps the Torah eternal
        and what keeps the congregation alive. 99

—Rabbi David ben Abi Zimra, medieval Spanish Jewish sage

🕮 My Torah portion is:

_____
FILL IN NAME OF TORAH PORTION, IN HEBREW AND/OR ENGLISH

It is from:

_____
FILL IN BOOK OF THE TORAH, IN HEBREW AND/OR ENGLISH   CHAPTER   VERSES

My favorite verse is:

_____
WRITE OUT THE VERSE IN HEBREW AND/OR ENGLISH

Place
Stamp
Here

**JEWISH LIGHTS PUBLISHING
SUNSET FARM OFFICES RTE 4
PO BOX 237
WOODSTOCK VT   05091-0237**

⫿⫿⫿⫿⫿⫿⫿⫿⫿⫿⫿⫿⫿⫿⫿⫿⫿⫿⫿⫿⫿⫿⫿⫿⫿⫿⫿⫿⫿⫿

VERSES

It relates to my life in this way:

_____

_____

_____

My Devar Torah

Print it out and attach it here.

Judaism says that thirteen is the age of spiritual and moral choices. Some rabbinic sources say that only upon turning thirteen is a youth first able to make mature choices, because then the child becomes endowed with both the *yetzer hara* (the evil inclination, which urges us to be selfish and not look at the moral issues behind our actions) and the *yetzer hatov* (the good inclination), the dueling forces that Jewish theology perceives are within each of us. Now, you can begin to ascend to the good and the holy, and start making ethical decisions.

What are some ethical and moral issues that you expect to confront over the next few years? Which Jewish principles do you hope to draw on when you make your choices about each? For example:

Shabbat: Honoring the Sabbath
Gemilut Chasadim: Acts of Loving-Kindness
Talmud Torah: The Study of Torah
Kedushat Halashon: The Holiness of Speech
Tzar Baalei Chayim: Noncruelty to Animals
Hidur P'nai Zakein: Honoring the Elderly
Kol Yisrael Arevim: All Jews Are Responsible for Each Other
Tikkun Atzmi: Repairing the Self
Tikkun Olam: Repairing the World

_____

_____

_____

_____

_____

_____

_____

_____

"Bar/Bat Mitzvah" literally means "one who is liable to fulfill the commandments." I understand this as:

_____

_____

_____

_____

_____

_____

The phrase "I am Jewish" means different things to different people. When I say, "I am Jewish," I'm saying:

_____

_____

_____

_____

_____

_____

66 In every interaction ...
         in any of my relationships,
      no matter what I do,
            I am a Jew. **99**

—Debbie Friedman, in *I Am Jewish*

From All
My Teachers
I Have
Gained
Wisdom

מכל
מלמדי
השכלתי

“As a teenager in my synagogue recently said:

'A Judaism
that doesn't ask you to make any changes in your life
is not Judaism.'

So instead of just 'coasting through' Judaism,
imagine a Judaism that asks us
to make changes in our lives.
Moreover, *demand* a Judaism
that requires such changes.
Anything less is not Judaism.”

—*For Kids—Putting God on Your Guest List*

“I had a teacher in the sixth grade
who knew how to make me feel good.
She had a saying that made me feel
like I could take on the world:

'You should be so proud of yourself.'”

—*The JGirl's Guide*

👁 **My rabbi(s):**

_____
NAME(S) OF RABBI(S)

Ask your rabbi(s) to answer below:

What Jewish values are most important to you? What special Jewish teachings do you want me to remember?

_____

_____

_____

_____

_____

👁 **My cantor(s):**

_____
NAME(S) OF CANTOR(S)

Ask your cantor(s) to answer below:

What Jewish values are most important to you? What special Jewish teachings do you want me to remember?

_____

_____

_____

_____

_____

❝ Get yourself a rabbi, and acquire for yourself a study companion. ❞

—Pirke Avot

👁 I have a special religious school teacher, director of education, or youth leader who has helped me grow up as a young Jew.

This person's name is:

_____

Ask this person to answer below:
What Jewish values are most important to you? What special Jewish teachings do you want me to remember?

_____

_____

_____

_____

👁 These are the names of the congregation leaders who participated in my ceremony:

_____

_____

Ask these congregation leaders to answer below:
Why do you love our synagogue? What do you love about Judaism? Why do you want Judaism to continue?

_____

_____

_____

_____

66 May your heart be filled
with intuition
and your words
be filled with insight. **99**

—Talmud

Come
Before God
with
Rejoicing

באו לפניו
ברננה

66 The scroll was returned to the ark
with song and procession,
and the service was resumed.
No thunder sounded,
no lightning struck.
The institution of bat mitzvah
had been born without incident,
and the rest of the day was all rejoicing. **99**

—Judith Kaplan Eisenstein, describing her May 1922
bat mitzvah ceremony (the first in North America)

66 May songs of praise
ever be upon your tongue
and your vision
a straight path before you. **99**

—Talmud

🔊 Who led the service?

_____

🔊 Who else said something special to me?

_____

I remember these words (from rabbis, cantors, or congregation leaders):

_____

_____

_____

_____

🔊 Who else did something special for me?

_____

What was done for me?

_____

Gift(s) I received from the congregation:

_____

_____

" In synagogue, I feel the presence of God
in the sounds of all of us
who have gathered to celebrate life together.
In synagogue, I know that I belong—
that my life matters to all these people.
I am touched by the lives of others,
and they are touched by me.**"**

—*Tough Questions Jews Ask*

Attach photographs of the rehearsal and/or ceremony.
Tell what is happening in each photograph.

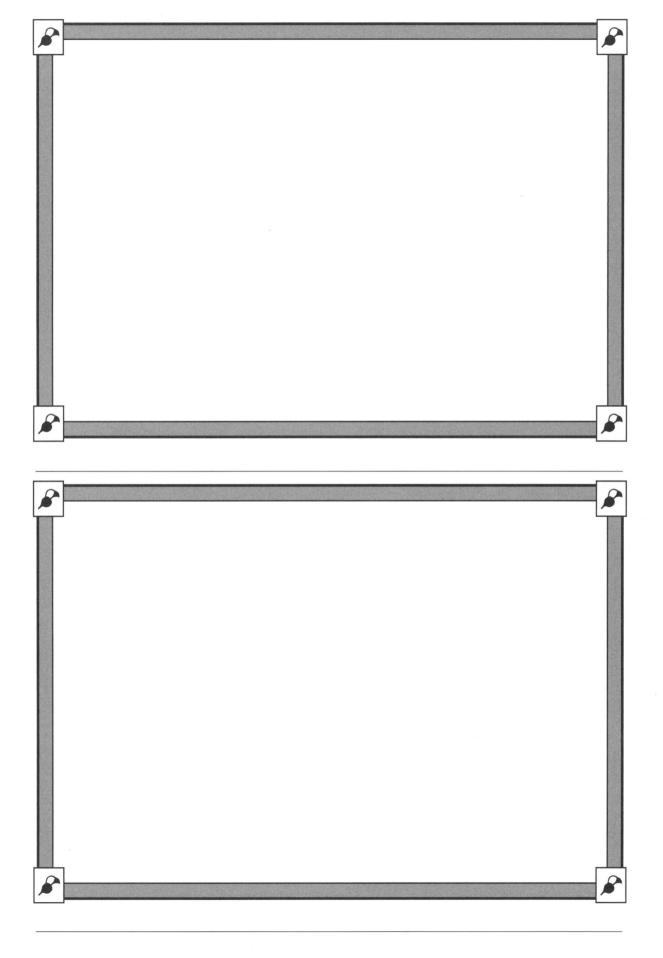

At the Shabbat dinner before my bar/bat mitzvah ceremony, the following people had special honors or offered special words:

_____

_____

_____

_____

_____

I remember that these are some of the things they said:

_____

_____

_____

_____

_____

_____

66 One thread links all the bar and bat mitzvah ceremonies
throughout history,
all the comings of age of every Jewish boy from Abraham on
and of every Jewish girl from Sarah on.
Bar and bat mitzvah means that you now are responsible for
fulfilling the *mitzvot* of Jewish ritual.
It is about growing up as a Jew.
It is about becoming a fuller member of the Jewish community.
It is about moral responsibility,
about connecting to Torah, to community, to God. **99**

—*For Kids—Putting God on Your Guest List*

🔑 I received some special gifts for my life as a Jewish adult:

_____ gave me a *tallit*.

_____ gave me a *kippah*.

_____ gave me *tefilin*.

_____ gave me _____.

_____ gave me _____.

_____ gave me _____.

If any of these objects have a special story, write about it here:

_____

_____

_____

_____

_____

❝ All relatives contributed
to the outfit
of the Bar Mitzvah boy. ❞

—Caption for a photograph of
a bar mitzvah boy in Poland in the 1930s,
taken by the famous photographer Roman Vishniac

Honors

Who opened the ark during the service?

_____

Who had *aliyot*?

_____   _____

_____   _____

_____   _____

_____   _____

Who did *hagbah* (lifting the Torah)? _____

Who did *gelilah* (dressing the Torah)? _____

Who held the Torah? _____

Who else had honors during the service? What were these honors?

_____   _____

_____   _____

Who did *Kiddush* at the celebration? _____

Who did *Motzi*? _____

> ❝ At such moments we understand the Torah blessing.
> *Baruch attah Adonai, notein hatorah,*
> 'Blessed are You, Adonai, Giver of the Torah.'
> God did not just give Torah at Sinai. God gives Torah today.
> This is Torah's magical potency that has spoken through the ages. ❞

—*Putting God on the Guest List*

To me, the most meaningful parts of the service were:

_____

_____

_____

_____

What prayer from the service did you find most meaningful?

Copy it from your prayerbook and attach it here.

The music or songs I found most meaningful were:

_____

_____

_____

66 There is an angel with a thousand heads.
Each head has a thousand mouths.
Each mouth has a thousand tongues.
Each tongue has a thousand songs.
Imagine the beauty of this angel's prayers. 99

—Rebbe Nachman of Breslov, Hasidic teacher

🖋 **This page is for your parent(s) to fill out.**

In traditional Judaism, parents say a prayer when their child becomes bar or bat mitzvah.

This is what it is:

ברוך שפטרני מענשו של זה

Baruch she-petarani me-onsho shel zeh.

"Blessed is the One Who has now freed me from responsibility for this child."

You are not freed from *all* responsibility for your new teenager's behavior, but how do you want your child to use his or her new maturity?

_____

_____

_____

_____

_____

_____

❝ An important part of becoming bar or bat mitzvah
is growing as an individual.
Ancient rabbis believed that the ultimate goal of the *mitzvot*
was nothing less than *letzaref haberiot*,
turning someone into a better person. ❞

—*For Kids—Putting God on Your Guest List*

Joy
and
Gladness

שמחה
וששון

66 The peak moments of life,
      when we experience the drama of passage,
have an uncanny way of bringing us home.
   They can take us out of exile
                and show us the Jerusalem of the soul.
      They remind us that our lives
   have a rhythm and a purpose. **99**

—Putting God on the Guest List

🏆 Attach your invitation here.

🏆 41

A place for your guests to sign or write their wishes for you.

_____

_____

_____

_____

_____

_____

_____

_____

_____

_____

_____

_____

_____

_____

_____

_____

_____

_____

_____

_____

_____

_____

_____

_____

_____

_____

_____

_____

_____

_____

_____

_____

_____

_____

_____

_____

_____

_____

_____

_____

_____

66 Prayer is a way to learn how to stop
and notice the miracles around us.
Prayer is a way to have a moment with God. **99**

—*Tough Questions Jews Ask*

_____

_____

_____

_____

_____

_____

_____

_____

_____

_____

_____

_____

_____

_____

_____

66 Torah continues into our own day.
As *Pirke Avot* (the ethical teachings of the ancient rabbis) says,
'Every day a voice goes forth from Sinai'—
every day, at least,
if we turn down the noise of the world
and train our ears to hear the truth
and the beauty of the Torah. **99**

—*For Kids—Putting God on Your Guest List*

Clear
a Pathway
through
the Wilderness
of Life

פנו דרך
במדבר

" The religious individual can never sit still.
He or she is always packing up the tent,
moving through the wilderness of life,
and remembering that there is
a Promised Land of the soul. **"**

—*Putting God on the Guest List*

" To be Jewish means to go forward,
to bring order where there is chaos.
It means both to cry out against injustice
and to act against it....
Judaism recognizes God in small acts of heroism,
in deeds of compassion and courage,
in the hands and hearts and voices
of those who work to bring healing
and justice to the world. **"**

—Rabbi Sandy Eisenberg Sasso, in *I Am Jewish*

My plans for my Jewish future: ✓

☐ To continue religious school
☐ To decide who my favorite Jewish authors are and to learn from them
☐ To join my synagogue youth group
☐ To volunteer in my Jewish community or synagogue
☐ To go to a Jewish summer camp
☐ To go on a trip to Israel

☐ _____

☐ _____

I plan to learn more about: ✓

☐ Jewish history
☐ The Holocaust (Shoah)
☐ Israel
☐ Women's contributions to Judaism
☐ Jewish prayer
☐ Jewish thought

☐ Social justice issues from a Jewish point of view
☐ Mysticism
☐ Meditation
☐ Jewish music
☐ Jewish art
☐ Jewish dance

☐ _____   ☐ _____

Mitzvot and acts of *tikkun olam* (repairing the world) that I want to do:

_____

_____

_____

_____

> **❝** Let young people know that
> every deed counts,
> that every word has power.
> Let them remember to build a life
> as if it were a work of art. **❞**

—Abraham Joshua Heschel,
twentieth-century Jewish theologian and philosopher

Helpful resources for keeping the spiritual meaning in bar and bat mitzvah.

Putting God on the Guest List, 3rd Edition: *How to Reclaim the Spiritual Meaning of Your Child's Bar or Bat Mitzvah*

By Rabbi Jeffrey K. Salkin (Reform)
Foreword by Rabbi Sandy Eisenberg Sasso (Reconstructionist)
Introduction by Rabbi William H. Lebeau (Conservative)

Helps people find core spiritual values in American Jewry's most misunderstood ceremony; shows how to make the event more spiritually meaningful.

"I hope every family planning a bar or bat mitzvah celebration reads Rabbi Salkin's book."
—Rabbi Harold S. Kushner, author of *When Bad Things Happen to Good People*

6 x 9, 224 pp, Quality PB, ISBN: 978-1-58023-222-7 $16.99;
HC, ISBN: 978-1-58023-260-9 $24.99
Also available: *Putting God on the Guest List Teacher's Guide*
8½ x 11, 48 pp, PB, ISBN: 978-1-58023-226-5 $8.99

For Kids—Putting God on Your Guest List, 2nd Edition
How to Claim the Spiritual Meaning of Your Bar or Bat Mitzvah

By Rabbi Jeffrey K. Salkin

An important resource for kids ages 11 and 12 to help them spiritually prepare for their bar/bat mitzvah.

"I would recommend this book to my friends, my younger brother and sister, my cousins, and everyone I know who will become bar or bat mitzvah."
—Joshua Zecher Ross, age 13

"We've used *Putting God on the Guest List* in our b'nai mitzvah program for many years. I've always wished for a companion book that could talk to the kids themselves. This is the book I've been waiting for!"
—Rabbi Laura Geller, Temple Emanuel, Beverly Hills, California

6 x 9, 144 pp, Quality PB, ISBN: 978-1-58023-308-8 $15.99

Bar/Bat Mitzvah Basics, 2nd Edition: *A Practical Family Guide to Coming of Age Together*

Edited by Cantor Helen Leneman
Foreword by Rabbi Jeffrey K. Salkin

A practical guide that gives families the information they need to manage the bar/bat mitzvah process with grace, joy and good sense.

6 x 9, 240 pp, Quality PB, ISBN: 978-1-58023-151-0 $18.95

I Am Jewish: *Personal Reflections Inspired by the Last Words of Daniel Pearl*

Edited by Judea and Ruth Pearl

Inspires Jewish people of all backgrounds to reflect upon and take pride in their identity.

6 x 9, 304 pp, Deluxe PB w/flaps
ISBN: 978-1-58023-259-3 $18.99
Also available: *I Am Jewish Teacher's Guide*
8½ x 11, 10 pp, PB, ISBN: 978-1-58023-219-7 $6.99;
or download a free copy at our website, www.jewishlights.com

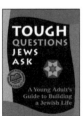

Tough Questions Jews Ask
A Young Adult's Guide to Building a Jewish Life

By Rabbi Edward Feinstein

What your rabbi probably never told you—about God, belief, the meaning of life and more—but could have, if you had only asked.

6 x 9, 160 pp, Quality PB, ISBN: 978-1-58023-139-8 $14.99
Also available: *Tough Questions Jews Ask Teacher's Guide*
8½ x 11, 72 pp, PB, ISBN: 978-1-58023-187-9 $8.95

The JGirl's Guide: *The Young Jewish Woman's Handbook for Coming of Age*

By Penina Adelman, Ali Feldman and Shulamit Reinharz

A first-of-its-kind book of practical, real-world advice using Judaism as a compass for the journey through adolescence.

6 x 9, 240 pp, Quality PB, ISBN: 978-1-58023-215-9 $14.99
Also available: *The JGirl's Teacher's and Parent's Guide*
8½ x 11, 56 pp, PB, ISBN: 978-1-58023-225-8 $8.99